QUESTIONS GOD ASKS

9 STUDIES FOR INDIVIDUALS OR GROUPS

LifeGuide®
BIBLE STUDIES

DALE LARSEN AND SANDY LARSEN

IVP Connect

An imprint of InterVarsity Press
Downers Grove, Illinois

InterVarsity Press
P.O. Box 1400, Downers Grove, IL 60515-1426
ivpress.com
email@ivpress.com

InterVarsity Press® is the book-publishing division of InterVarsity Christian Fellowship/USA®, a movement of students and faculty active on campus at hundreds of universities, colleges, and schools of nursing in the United States of America, and a member movement of the International Fellowship of Evangelical Students. For information about local and regional activities, visit intervarsity.org.

LifeGuide® is a registered trademark of InterVarsity Christian Fellowship.

All Scripture quotations, unless otherwise indicated, are taken from The Holy Bible, New International Version®, NIV®. Copyright © 1973, 1978, 1984, 2011 by Biblica, Inc.™ Used by permission of Zondervan. All rights reserved worldwide. www.zondervan.com. The "NIV" and "New International Version" are trademarks registered in the United States Patent and Trademark Office by Biblica, Inc.™

While any stories in this book are true, some names and identifying information may have been changed to protect the privacy of individuals.

Cover design: Cindy Kiple
Interior design: Jeanna Wiggins and Daniel van Loon
Cover image: oceanscape: © Lisa5201 / iStock / Getty Images Plus

ISBN 978-0-8308-3078-7 (print)
ISBN 978-0-8308-6432-4 (digital)

Printed in the United States of America ∞

InterVarsity Press is committed to ecological stewardship and to the conservation of natural resources in all our operations. This book was printed using sustainably sourced paper.

P	17	16	15	14	13	12	11	10	9	8	7	6	5	4	3	2	1
Y	32	31	30	29	28	27	26	25	24	23	22	21	20	19	18		

CONTENTS

Getting the Most Out of *Questions God Asks* 5

ONE Where Are You? 9
GENESIS 3:1-13

TWO What Is That in Your Hand? 12
EXODUS 4:1-5

THREE Why Are You Crying Out to Me? 16
EXODUS 14:5-25

FOUR Stand Up! What Are You Doing Down on Your Face? 20
JOSHUA 7:1-15

FIVE What Are You Doing Here? 24
1 KINGS 19:1-18

SIX Why Do You Complain, Jacob? 28
ISAIAH 40:27-31; 41:8-10

SEVEN Can These Bones Live? 32
EZEKIEL 37:1-14

EIGHT Is It Right for You to Be Angry? 36
JONAH 4:1-11

NINE Is It a Time for You Yourselves to Be Living in Your
Paneled Houses, While This House Remains a Ruin? 40
HAGGAI 1:1-15

Leader's Notes 45

GETTING THE
MOST OUT OF
QUESTIONS GOD ASKS

On a recent camping trip, we drove past a church with a banner out front that said, "Got questions? God has them too."

Our first reaction was, "What? Like God wonders about stuff or is puzzled by anything."

Then one of us thought of a question God asked Abraham, and the other thought of a question God asked Moses, and we rode along volleying biblical questions back and forth. Several miles later we had decided that (1) the banner was correct and (2) "Questions God Asks" would make an intriguing and valuable Bible study.

Most of us expend a lot of energy asking the Lord questions and demanding answers. Why did such-and-such happen? Where should I live or work or study or go to escape my problems? How long will this awkward situation continue? Why didn't you help me the way I expected? Most of us give less attention to the questions God asks us. This study guide explores nine of those questions found in the Old Testament. While each question is only one verse, each study unfolds the larger context of the question: immediate circumstances, background, identity of the person being questioned, the person's response, and the apparent results.

It is still reasonable to wonder what we wondered when we saw that banner: Why would God, who knows everything, ask human beings anything? Here are several possibilities:

- To confront people with himself—both his holiness and the resources of his grace.
- To keep up communication with humanity even in the midst of rebellion.
- To invite people to be honest with him.

- To urge people to be honest with themselves.
- To get people thinking about reality rather than illusion.

You may be surprised that this study guide is titled *Questions God Asks* rather than *Questions God Asked*. God asked these questions of people many centuries ago, but we believe through conscience, Scripture, and circumstances God still asks us these same questions today. May we always be brave enough to answer honestly.

What about the banner in front of that church? What did it mean? Our best guess is that it was meant to stir up interest in a sermon series on the questions of God. Sadly, we cannot recall the name of the church or even the name of the town where we saw the banner. But whoever put it up, wherever it was, thank you. We hope it brought good results for your church, your community, and the kingdom of God.

SUGGESTIONS FOR INDIVIDUAL STUDY

1. As you begin each study, pray that God will speak to you through his Word.

2. Read the introduction to the study and respond to the personal reflection question or exercise. This is designed to help you focus on God and on the theme of the study.

3. Each study deals with a particular passage so that you can delve into the author's meaning in that context. Read and re-read the passage to be studied. The questions are written using the language of the New International Version, so you may wish to use that version of the Bible. The New Revised Standard Version is also recommended.

4. This is an inductive Bible study, designed to help you discover for yourself what Scripture is saying. The study includes three types of questions. Observation questions ask about the basic facts: who, what, when, where, and how. Interpretation questions delve into the meaning of the passage. Application questions help you discover the implications of the text for growing in Christ. These three keys unlock the treasures of Scripture.

Write your answers to the questions in the spaces provided or in a personal journal. Writing can bring clarity and deeper understanding of yourself and of God's Word.

5. It might be good to have a Bible dictionary handy. Use it to look up any unfamiliar words, names, or places.

6. Use the prayer suggestion to guide you in thanking God for what you have learned and to pray about the applications that have come to mind.

7. You may want to go on to the suggestion under "Now or Later," or you may want to use that idea for your next study.

SUGGESTIONS FOR MEMBERS OF A GROUP STUDY

1. Come to the study prepared. Follow the suggestions for individual study mentioned above. You will find that careful preparation will greatly enrich your time spent in group discussion.

2. Be willing to participate in the discussion. The leader of your group will not be lecturing. Instead, he or she will be encouraging the members of the group to discuss what they have learned. The leader will be asking the questions that are found in this guide.

3. Stick to the topic being discussed. Your answers should be based on the verses that are the focus of the discussion and not on outside authorities such as commentaries or speakers. These studies focus on a particular passage of Scripture. Only rarely should you refer to other portions of the Bible. This allows for everyone to participate in in-depth study on equal ground.

4. Be sensitive to the other members of the group. Listen attentively when they describe what they have learned. You may be surprised by their insights! Each question assumes a variety of answers. Many questions do not have "right" answers, particularly questions that aim at meaning or application. Instead the questions push us to explore the passage more thoroughly.

When possible, link what you say to the comments of others. Also, be affirming whenever you can. This will encourage some of the more hesitant members of the group to participate.

5. Be careful not to dominate the discussion. We are sometimes so eager to express our thoughts that we leave too little opportunity for others to respond. By all means participate! But allow others to also.

6. Expect God to teach you through the passage being discussed and through the other members of the group. Pray that you will have an enjoyable and profitable time together, but also that as a result of the study you will find ways that you can take action individually or as a group.

7. Remember that anything said in the group is considered confidential and should not be discussed outside the group unless specific permission is given to do so.

8. If you are the group leader, you will find additional suggestions at the back of the guide.

ONE

WHERE ARE YOU?

Genesis 3:1-13

Campers in the northern United States and Canada are always unnerved the first time they hear the cries of the common loon. This large black-and-white water bird makes several distinct calls. The yodel is a raucous territorial claim. The tremolo alarm call sounds like maniacal laughter. Eeriest of all is the loon's wail, which sounds like a human voice calling, "Where *are* you?" In fact that is what wailing loons are asking, for they use the wail to locate each other.

So far as we know, "Where are you?" was the first question God posed to humanity. It came at a crisis point between human beings and their Creator God.

Group Discussion. Besides physical location, what are some other ways to answer the question, "Where are you?"

Personal Reflection. When and why have you not wanted to reveal where you were, either physically or in some other way?

God placed the first man and woman in a perfect garden and gave them only one prohibition: "You are free to eat from any tree in the garden; but you must not eat from the tree of the knowledge of good and evil, for when you eat from it you will certainly die" (Genesis 2:16-17). We don't know how long it was before the crafty serpent approached with temptation, but the serpent managed to plant mistrust in Eve's mind, with tragic results. *Read Genesis 3:1-13.*

1. Why did the man hide (v. 8)? The obvious answer is, because he had sinned. But why was he afraid to face God after his sin?

2. God already knew exactly where the man was. Why then would he ask, "Where are you?" (v. 9).

3. What are some implications of the fact that God "called" to the man as opposed to "said"?

4. Where *was* Adam? Physically he was still in Eden. Apparently it was still a perfect place; the curse and the expulsion from Eden comes later in verses 14-24. But how did Eden suddenly *feel* like a different place?

5. In the space of verses 7-10, how has the relationship between God and humanity radically changed?

6. In that same passage, how has the relationship between God and humanity remained unchanged?

7. Adam gave an honest answer even as he tried to hide from God (v. 10). Adam was in a conflicted spiritual and emotional state, with both honesty and avoidance going on at the same time. In what ways can Christians sympathize?

8. The man and woman couldn't avoid God, but they felt compelled to try. What are some "trees" people try to hide behind in order to avoid God?

9. As Christians we have not gone back to Eden, but we are in a forgiven and restored relationship with God. Then why do we sometimes still try to avoid God?

10. If right now God called to you and asked, "Where are you?," how would you answer?

11. What will you do this week to be more open with God?

 Pray that you will fearlessly face the Lord, be honest about your sin, and accept his mercy in Christ.

NOW OR LATER

Study Psalm 139. In this psalm the writer asks, "Where can I go from your Spirit?" and acknowledges that it is impossible to go anywhere beyond the sight of the Lord.

Because of the gospel, Christian believers do not need to fear God's presence. In fact Scripture encourages us to boldly approach the Lord. Study Hebrews 4:14-16 and 10:19-25, where we find assurance that we can approach God with confidence because Christ our high priest has gone ahead of us.

TWO

WHAT IS THAT IN YOUR HAND?

Exodus 4:1-5

H ow would you like to teach the youth Sunday school class?"
The question could have been put more accurately as a blunt
statement: "We're desperate for somebody to teach the youth Sunday
school class, and you're the only person available to do it." Sandy had
never taught Sunday school before, but she had a good relationship
with the high schoolers in our small church, so she said yes.

The youth class turned out to include everybody in the church from
roughly age twelve to twenty-two. There was no curriculum suitable for
such a wide age range, so Sandy turned to what she had: a pretty good
knowledge of the Bible, lots of paper, and the church mimeograph ma-
chine (she was the church administrative assistant). For two years she
cranked out weekly lessons, each lesson based on the discussion of the
week before. Those ink-blotched experimental lessons eventually
became the basis of our decision to go into full-time writing.

When a need arises, sometimes you have to use what you have on
hand. When Moses met God at the burning bush, God told him to use
what he had *in* his hand—his ordinary shepherd's staff. That staff went
on to play a significant role in the Israelites' exodus from Egypt.

Group Discussion. When have you felt inadequate?

Personal Reflection. When have you felt inadequate to do something
you felt God was calling you to do?

Moses, child of Hebrew slaves in Egypt, was rescued from certain
death and raised as the son of Pharaoh's daughter. As an adult he tried

to intervene for his people and had to flee into the Sinai desert, where for the next forty years he worked as a shepherd. God met him in a flaming bush and commissioned him to return to Egypt and lead his people out of slavery and into the land of promise. Scan Exodus 3. Note especially God's summons to Moses in Exodus 3:10. Moses raised several objections, which the Lord answered (Exodus 3:11-15). *Read Exodus 4:1-5.*

1. At this point what was uppermost in Moses' mind (v. 1)?

2. How did the Lord unexpectedly change the focus of Moses' attention (v. 2)?

3. What is the logical connection between Moses' objection and God's question?

4. To Moses at that moment, what was the significance of his staff?

5. God ordered Moses to do a simple act of obedience: "Throw it on the ground" (v. 3). How was the result different from anything Moses might have expected to happen?

6. When God told Moses to pick up the snake by the tail, what probably went through Moses' mind?

7. What was the purpose of the demonstration with the staff (v. 5)?

8. When have you seen the Lord use ordinary objects or circumstances to do something remarkable, perhaps even miraculous?

9. Identify some ordinary everyday "staffs" you have "in your hand." Some possibilities could be: material possessions, financial resources, schedule flexibility, talents and skills, space (home or yard), vehicles, friends or family or church networks, special sensitivities, or latent interests.

10. Which one of your "staffs" would be hardest for you to throw down and release control over?

11. We know now what a significant part Moses' staff played in the exodus and in the wilderness journey, but at this point the Lord did not reveal any of that to Moses. He only promised that the Israelites (not even the Egyptians yet) would believe that the Lord had really appeared to Moses. Moses was still very much in the dark about where all this was going. But he did throw down the staff and pick up the snake by the tail. This week, what will you figuratively throw down and let God take control of?

Identify specific steps you will take in order to do that.

 Pray that you will recognize and surrender the resources the Lord has given you and let him use them to carry out his will.

NOW OR LATER

Study other places in Scripture where ordinary objects become the means of God's miraculous working:

- Salt in a new bowl (2 Kings 2:19-22)
- Morning sun on water (2 Kings 3:1-23)
- Jars of oil (2 Kings 4:1-7)
- A sundial (Isaiah 38:1-8)
- Handkerchiefs and aprons (Acts 19:11-12)

THREE

WHY ARE YOU CRYING OUT TO ME?

Exodus 14:5-25

The Russian play *Uncle Vanya* by Anton Chekhov is usually billed as a comedy; but if you see it, don't expect any belly laughs. Like much Russian drama, *Uncle Vanya* consists of a lot of unhappy people standing around talking about how unhappy they are but never taking any action to make things better. You want to stand up in the audience and yell, "Shut up and *do* something!"

The characters in *Uncle Vanya* are trapped in inactivity because the playwright has put so many hopeless words into their mouths. Chronic complaining immobilizes us. It is easier to gripe than to take action to change things.

At a time when things looked desperately hopeless, Moses cried out to the Lord. The Lord surprised him by telling him to stop crying out and start moving forward.

Group Discussion. If a friend said to you, "I feel stuck and can't do anything about my situation," what would you say?

Personal Reflection. Do you agree or disagree that sometimes, in some situations, we have no choices and no options? Why do you answer as you do?

Equipped with the "staff of God," Moses and his brother, Aaron, went to the Egyptian pharaoh to demand the release of the Hebrew slaves. It took a series of devastating plagues on Egypt before pharaoh finally allowed the slaves to leave. Shortly afterward, pharaoh realized he had lost his main labor force and sent his army after them. *Read Exodus 14:5-14.*

1. Why did the Israelites have good reason to be terrified (vv. 7, 9)?

2. What options appeared to be open to them?

3. Think of a time when you felt stuck, and you desperately asked the Lord to help you. What happened as a result?

4. How did Moses try to encourage the people (vv. 13-14)?

5. If you were one of the Israelites and heard Moses' words of reassurance, how do you think you would react, and why?

6. *Read Exodus 14:15-25.* From verse 15, what do you suppose Moses might have been feeling that he had *not* expressed publicly?

7. Throughout Scripture people cry out to the Lord, and he answers. Moses was sent to deliver the Israelites in response to their crying out in slavery (Exodus 2:23-25). As Pharaoh's army approached, the trapped Israelites cried out to God (Exodus 14:10). Then why does the Lord abruptly cut off Moses' cries for help (v. 15)?

8. Instead of crying out, what was Moses told to do, and with what promise (vv. 15-18)?

9. What were the results of this new course of action (vv. 19-25)?

10. Moses had a problem, he cried out to God, and God spoke to him in some understandable way. We have our own problems, and we cry out to God. What are some ways we hear from God in response to our prayers?

11. What is the connection between closeness with God and knowing what God wishes you to do?

12. The Lord told Moses, "Tell the Israelites to move on" (v. 15). How might the Lord be saying to you now, "Move on!" or in other words, "Get going! Take action!"

13. What will you do to obey the Lord's promptings?

 First of all, pray for a closer relationship with God, which will put you into the path of his plans for you. Then pray for wisdom to know when to wait and when to move forward.

NOW OR LATER

Study other Scriptures in which people are reluctant to do something and the Lord tells them to get moving anyway:

- 2 Chronicles 20:1-30
- Acts 9:1-19
- Acts 10:1-23

Moses received direction from hearing God's unmistakable voice. Normally, we are not so privileged. To help you think further about discerning God's will, here are some resources from a range of perspectives:

- *Decision Making and the Will of God: A Biblical Alternative to the Traditional View* by Garry Friesen
- *Discovering God's Will in Your Life* by Lloyd John Ogilvie
- *God's Will: Finding Guidance for Everyday Decisions* by J. I. Packer and Carolyn Nystrom
- *God's Will, God's Best for Your Life* by Josh McDowell and Kevin Johnson
- *Listening to God in Times of Choice: The Art of Discerning God's Will* by Gordon T. Smith
- *A Slow and Certain Light: Thoughts on the Guidance of God* by Elisabeth Elliot

FOUR

STAND UP!
WHAT ARE YOU DOING
DOWN ON YOUR FACE?

Joshua 7:1-15

W̲e were canoeing a small river in northern Wisconsin, heading
for its outlet into Lake Superior. Our friend was alongside in
his kayak. We had not been on this stretch of water before, but our
friend's map showed that this part of the river had no serious rapids or
obstructions. What could go wrong?

Suddenly the water ahead took on the sinister form of a straight line.
We all back-paddled and paused to take a closer look. Not far ahead the
river cascaded over a concrete barrier. It was a low-head dam designed
to keep invasive sea lampreys from coming upstream to spawn. In a
profound understatement our friend remarked, "This isn't on the map."

On the rivers of our lives we encounter a lot of obstacles not on the
map, if we had a map in the first place. At those stressful times, the Lord
may ask us pointed and revealing questions.

Group Discussion. What are some unexpected difficulties that drive
people to seek answers from God?

Personal Reflection. When have you seen a sure thing abruptly go wrong?

The Israelites escaped from slavery in Egypt, spent a generation in
the wilderness, and finally crossed the Jordan River to take possession
of Canaan. They attacked and defeated Jericho in obedience to the
Lord's careful instructions (Joshua 6). Jericho was to be destroyed, and

nothing was to be looted, except that silver, gold, and articles of bronze and iron were to be set apart for the Lord's treasury (Joshua 6:18-19). *Read Joshua 7:1-10.*

1. The writer of Judges reveals in advance that there is secret sin in the Israelite camp (v. 1), but Joshua and the elders do not yet know about it. How does the attack on Ai go terribly wrong?

2. Before the attack on Jericho, Joshua met the "commander of the army of the LORD" and "fell facedown to the ground in reverence" (Joshua 5:14). Then it was a posture of worship and awe; now he is "facedown to the ground" before the ark of the LORD in desperate prayer and petition. God asks Joshua why he has fallen on his face. Why *is* Joshua on his face?

3. Paraphrase Joshua's complaints in each part of his desperate plea (vv. 7-9).

4. When have you asked similar questions or made similar statements in the face of an unexpected bad turn of events?

5. The Lord's sharp command "Stand up!" (v. 10) was certainly meant physically: get up off the ground and onto your feet! How might the action of standing up physically lead Joshua to stand up in other ways?

6. *Read Joshua 7:11-15.* Joshua begged for an explanation, and the Lord gave him an immediate and clear answer. Identify the specific sin(s) committed.

7. Achan was singled out and specifically identified in verse 1. Then why do you think the Lord says, "Israel has sinned" (v. 11)?

8. How can the sin of one person affect an entire church, Christian fellowship, or ministry?

9. When have you been facedown before the Lord—literally or figuratively—asking him "Why?" and then you realized that the "Why?" was because of sin, either someone else's or your own, or both? Share with the group if you are comfortable.

What did you do with your realization, and what were the results?

10. Where and how do you need to step-up and take responsibility for things that seem to be going wrong in your church fellowship, your family, or in your own life?

11. What steps will you take this week to help repair those situations?

 Consider ways sin may be harming your relationships or the relationships within your fellowship, family, or another group. If the sins are your own, confess them honestly before God and accept his forgiveness. If the sins are those of someone else, pray about how you might humbly and lovingly confront the offender.

NOW OR LATER

After Achan's sin was dealt with (Joshua 7:16-26), Israel was told to attack Ai again and this time not to be afraid or discouraged. Study the resultant successful campaign in Joshua 8:1-29.

Study Hebrews 12:4-17 and Deuteronomy 29:16-28. Both passages caution the people of God to stay faithful to him and to avoid letting any bitter root poison their relationships with the Lord and with each other.

FIVE

WHAT ARE YOU DOING HERE?

1 Kings 19:1-18

All kinds of difficult things happen to us with no warning and no chance to prepare. We find ourselves lost in a strange city, forced into early retirement, a parent of triplets, not a parent at all, disabled by an accident, rejected by a lifelong friend—whatever it is, we weren't ready for it. We look around and ask, "How did I get into this situation? Can't I take a break and lie low for a while?"

The prophet Elijah shared those feelings of confusion and the desire to escape after what was probably his greatest victory. Even in his state of withdrawal, he was not beyond the reach of God's care and mercy.

Group Discussion. After an outstanding success, why do we need to be vigilant about our emotional and spiritual lives?

Personal Reflection. When and why have you wanted to withdraw and not face reality? What did you do, with what results?

Ahab, one of the worst kings of Israel, "did more to arouse the anger of the LORD, the God of Israel, than did all the kings of Israel before him" (1 Kings 16:33). Ahab married the idolater Jezebel and set up an altar for Baal, the fertility god supposedly responsible for lightning and storms. Immediately after denouncing Ahab, the Bible introduces the prophet Elijah, who declares that there will be no rain until he gives the word. In the third year of drought, Elijah sets up a dramatic contest between Baal and the Lord; the Lord of course wins, and then rain comes at last. Jezebel and Ahab should be grateful for the rain which ends a disastrous famine. Instead, they are furious that their god has been proved false.

WHAT ARE YOU DOING HERE?   25

Jezebel swears to kill Elijah, and Elijah flees into the wilderness as far as Horeb (Mt. Sinai). *Read 1 Kings 19:1-18.*

1. Trace the stages of Elijah's withdrawal from Jezreel to Mt. Horeb (vv. 1-9).

2. How would you explain Elijah's prayer (and his mental and emotional state) in verse 4?

3. Elijah prayed to die. Far from taking his life, what did the Lord do instead (vv. 5-8)?

4. The Lord asked, "What are you doing here, Elijah?" (v. 9). Would you say Elijah's response (v. 10) was an answer to the question or not? Why do you say that?

5. How would you describe Elijah's mood and attitude as he answered the Lord?

6. In what circumstances have you shared Elijah's feelings?

7. What appears to be the purpose of what happened in verses 11-12?

If you were Elijah, how do you think you would react to what happens?

8. The Lord had told Elijah to "go out and stand on the mountain in the presence of the LORD" (v. 11). After several dramatic natural events, there was "a gentle whisper" (v. 12). Elijah heard the same question he had heard before. Would you expect Elijah to answer differently this time, or not? Why?

9. How did the Lord give Elijah a reason to get out of the cave (vv. 15-18)?

10. When and how has the Lord encouraged you to come out of hiding by giving you a purpose and a job to do?

11. What specific step will you take this week to face difficult circumstances with the help and strength of the Lord?

 Pray that you will walk forward boldly into a situation you have been shrinking back from in fear.

||||||||||||||||||||||||| NOW OR LATER |||||||||||||||||||||||||

Study any or all of these Scripture passages, which are pleas for the Lord's help in a crisis:

- 2 Kings 19:9-19
- Psalm 5
- Psalm 17
- Psalm 25
- Psalm 35
- Psalm 69

SIX

WHY DO YOU COMPLAIN, JACOB?

Isaiah 40:27-31; 41:8-10

W hy don't people respond to messages anymore? That may be an exaggeration, but not much. Do an internet search for "Why don't people call you back?" or "Why don't people reply to emails?" and you will get hundreds of hits from frustrated message senders. A writer for *Psychology Today* theorizes three reasons people fail to get back to us: (1) there are too many different kinds of messages out there, (2) people are too busy, and (3) people are lazy and would rather avoid the hard stuff.*

If it is disappointing to have a business associate or a friend ignore our messages, it is devastating to feel that God ignores our prayers. The people of God in exile in a hostile nation must have felt that God had disregarded or even forgotten them. The prophet Isaiah countered such discouragement with words of hope.

Group Discussion. What could make people feel that God is ignoring them?

Personal Reflection. Why do we expect the Lord to pay attention to our troubles and care about what happens to us?

After Solomon's death his kingdom was split in two: Israel in the north with its capital in Samaria, and Judah in the south with its capital

---

*Victor Lipman, "3 Reasons That No One Replies to Your Messages Anymore," *Psychology Today*, August 21, 2015, www.psychologytoday.com/blog/mind-the-manager/201508/3 -reasons-no-one-replies-your-messages-anymore.

in Jerusalem. Assyria conquered the Northern Kingdom in 722 BC and later looked south to threaten Judah. Although some outlying areas fell, the Lord miraculously spared Jerusalem in the time of King Hezekiah (Isaiah 36–37).

Some time after that deliverance, Hezekiah welcomed envoys from the kingdom of Babylon. The prophet Isaiah warned that Babylon would someday invade and conquer Judah (Isaiah 39). This happened in 586 BC after a long series of Babylonian sieges against Jerusalem. The city wall was broken down, the temple was destroyed, the temple furnishings were looted, and thousands of Jews were deported to Babylon with only the poorest left behind (2 Kings 25:11-12). The book of Lamentations expresses the desolate state of Jerusalem. Scripture is clear that the Babylonian conquest happened because the Jews had consistently rebelled against the Lord (2 Chronicles 36:5-21).

Beginning in Isaiah 40, the prophet looks ahead to the time when the Babylonian exile will end and the Jews will return to their homeland. Scan Isaiah 40, paying special attention to the contrast between the Lord's strength and the weakness of other powers. Many passages in Isaiah 40:1-11 are quoted in Handel's *Messiah* and are taken as prophecies of Christ's coming. They also point to an intermediate fulfillment in the Jews' return from exile, which began with the decree of Cyrus of Persia in 538 BC. *Read Isaiah 40:27-31.*

1. In this passage the Lord himself speaks through Isaiah. In your own words, what did the Lord ask Jacob and Israel—that is, the Jewish people (v. 27)?

2. Why would living in exile lead the Jews to think this way?

3. Recall that the exile happened because Judah disregarded the Lord (2 Chronicles 36:15-19). How does that fact affect how you see their complaints?

4. Think of a time when you complained that the Lord did not seem to be paying attention to your troubles. To what extent had you gotten yourself into your difficulties?

5. The Lord did not say, O Jacob, O Israel, you shouldn't complain this way. Instead he asked them *why* they complained in such a way. How does the question strengthen what the Lord wanted to communicate to them?

6. Verse 28 begins with two more brief questions, or one question asked in two different ways. What difference would it make for the exiled Jews to be reassured that God is the everlasting Creator?

7. Identify all the references to strength or power in verses 29-31. What is the relationship between the Lord's strength and the "hope" of verse 31?

8. *Read Isaiah 41:8-10.* The Lord again addressed Israel and Jacob—the Jewish people. What words and phrases did he use to remind the Jewish people of their history with him?

9. What parts of this passage would be most likely to turn the exiles' despair into faith?

10. What parts of this passage most inspire your faith right now?

11. What is one thing you will do this week to doubt less and trust more in the Lord?

 Pray that when you feel the Lord isn't paying attention to your prayers, you will remember that he does hear, he does care, and he is powerful to come to your aid.

NOW OR LATER

Choose something to serve as a reminder that God hears your prayers and wants to help you, for example, a physical object or a Scripture verse on a card, perhaps Isaiah 41:10. Place the reminder where you will see it often. Each time you see it, consciously thank God for his concern for you.

Study Psalms 42, 43, and 44, in which the writer honestly expresses frustration at God's silence, yet also expresses faith that God will come to the rescue.

SEVEN

CAN THESE BONES LIVE?

Ezekiel 37:1-14

W hen Sandy was in elementary school, she and her friends were frightened out of their wits by the Vincent Price movie *House on Haunted Hill*. Years later, in an article about the movie, she was surprised to read a plot summary. Plot? It had a plot? She couldn't remember any story line to the movie, only that it was terrifying.

There was one disappointment in *House on Haunted Hill*. The advertising promised an "Emergo" effect in which, at some key point in the movie, a skeleton would fly out over the heads of the audience. No skeleton appeared. Maybe that was better. A swooping skeleton would have induced even more nightmares in that group of young friends.

Skeletons unsettle us because they indicate death. If you see a skeleton, it means the person is no longer alive. For the prophet Ezekiel, a valley of scattered skeletons spoke only of death—until God showed him a vision of a miraculous return to life.

Group Discussion. What symbolizes death for you? What symbolizes life?

Personal Reflection. When has God changed an apparently hopeless situation into a hopeful one for you?

As Isaiah had warned, the Babylonians under Nebuchadnezzar attacked Judah and began to forcibly deport Jewish captives to Babylon. The priest Ezekiel was one of those early exiles. In his thirtieth year, which was the fifth year of the exile, he received dramatic visions from the Lord (Ezekiel 1:1-3). He had subsequent visions over the next years.

In the twelfth year of the exile he received shocking firsthand news that the city of Jerusalem had fallen (Ezekiel 33:21-22).

Up to chapter 34 of Ezekiel's prophecy, his messages to the Jewish exiles are filled with warnings about sin and calls for repentance. In chapters 34 and 36 the tone begins to change as the Lord sends encouraging messages about restoration and homecoming. By the time we come to the vision of the valley of bones in chapter 37, a momentum is established of promises for future restoration. *Read Ezekiel 37:1-10.*

1. What series of remarkable events took place in verses 1-2?

2. What might have been Ezekiel's impressions and reactions to what he was shown in verses 1-2?

3. When the Lord asked, "Son of man, can these bones live?" Ezekiel gave a rather indirect answer (v. 3). Why do you think he answered in that way?

4. The Lord gave Ezekiel a startling assignment in verses 4-6. What were the promised results?

5. Ezekiel obeyed the Lord and spoke to the bones and then to the breath. What happened in the two stages of his prophesying (vv. 7-10)?

6. What do you think the events of verses 7-10 looked and sounded like?

7. *Read Ezekiel 37:11-14.* How did the Lord interpret for Ezekiel what he had just seen?

8. Right then, how and why did Israel's situation seem as hopeless as a valley of dry bones?

9. The Lord quoted Israel's pessimistic view of the future (v. 11). How was Ezekiel instructed to inject hope into their pessimism (vv. 12-14)?

10. How did the Lord answer his own question ("Can these bones live?")? Not just that he answered yes, but how did he go about answering?

11. This Scripture's application to our own lives is tricky because we don't know for sure which situations we should see as hopeful (the Lord intends to breathe new life into them) and which are not in his purposes for us (either they're bad ideas or just not in his timing now). In any case, what personal connection do you feel with Ezekiel's experience?

12. In what areas do you need wisdom to know whether to hope for specific change or to back off from pushing for change?

13. What hopeful action will you take this week to place your hope in the Lord rather than in circumstances?

 Whether or not specific outcomes are in the Lord's plan for us, we can have hope in him and in his good purposes. Pray for an attitude of expectancy to be always on the lookout for God's good work in your life.

NOW OR LATER

Study John 5:16-30, in which Jesus says that a time is coming when the dead will hear his voice and will be raised to life, whether to eternal life or to condemnation, and that he has been given this authority by the Father.

Study Romans 8:18-27, in which Paul expresses the tension between ultimate hope and present suffering.

EIGHT

IS IT RIGHT FOR YOU TO BE ANGRY?

Jonah 4:1-11

At a church we attended some time ago, there was a bit of dead time between Sunday school and the worship service, so we suggested having a coffee and fellowship time. *No, no, no!* The idea was met with a stormy outburst of negativity. Apparently there were unresolved sore feelings in that church over coffee hours of the past. We dropped the subject, but we never got any explanation.

People get mad for strange reasons. Or more accurately, people get mad for perfectly good reasons that only they understand. We may find their anger bizarre, but if we could see inside their minds and hearts, we would comprehend why they react as they do.

Group Discussion. What feels bad about anger? What feels good about it?

Personal Reflection. When have you felt most justified at being angry?

Nineveh was the capital of the ancient Assyrian empire. Today its ruins are across the Tigris River from the city of Mosul in Iraq. About sixty years before the time of Jonah, Assyria humiliated Israel; an Assyrian stone obelisk depicts King Jehu's disgrace. By Jonah's time Assyria's power had waned somewhat. Assyria would regain strength and eventually conquer Israel in 722 BC (2 Kings 18:9-12).

The Lord called Jonah to "go to the great city of Nineveh and preach against it." Instead, Jonah fled to the Mediterranean port of Joppa and boarded a ship bound for Tarshish (Jonah 1:1-3). Tarshish was possibly in modern Spain near Gibraltar, but wherever it was, we can assume it was as far away from Nineveh as possible. The Lord intervened, and

Jonah went to Nineveh after all, where his preaching led to repentance. Instead of taking pleasure in his success, the prophet got mad. *Read Jonah 4:1-11.*

1. How do verses 1-3 shed light on Jonah's attempted escape from the Lord's call to go to Nineveh?

2. How did Jonah answer (or not answer) the Lord's question in verse 4?

3. Putting aside for now whether Jonah was justified in being angry, why *was* he angry and at whom?

4. Jonah sat down to observe the city (v. 5). What might he have been waiting and watching for?

5. Whose sin has made you angry? If you are willing, please share your answer with the group.

6. What do you think makes the difference, if there is one, between justified and unjustified anger?

7. As Jonah waited, the Lord caused several things to happen (vv. 6-8). What were their effects on Jonah?

8. Several times Jonah was even at the point of asking God to take his life (vv. 3, 8). If he was so miserable being angry, why do you think he still held on to his anger?

9. Sometimes we want God to be merciful to people who have done wrong; other times we want them to get what they deserve. What makes us feel one way or the other?

10. In verse 9 the Lord asked Jonah a more specific form of his original question in verse 4. This time Jonah answered directly. Do you think his answer is an improvement on his previous nonanswer or not? Why?

11. How did the Lord explain his mercy toward Nineveh (vv. 10-11)?

12. The book of Jonah ends abruptly with the Lord asking another question (v. 11). How do you react to this unusual conclusion to the book?

13. What steps will you take to let go of unjustified anger in a specific area (or toward a specific person) and be merciful as the Lord is merciful? If you are comfortable, share your response with the group.

Thank God for the person or people who first brought the gospel to you. Consider how your life would be different if they had fled in the opposite direction instead.

NOW OR LATER

Meditate on these Scriptures concerning anger, and write your responses to them:

- Proverbs 22:24-25
- 1 Corinthians 13:4-7
- Ephesians 4:25-27
- James 1:19-21

IS IT A TIME FOR YOU YOURSELVES TO BE LIVING IN YOUR PANELED HOUSES, WHILE THIS HOUSE REMAINS A RUIN?

Haggai 1:1-15

Why do we procrastinate? Blogger Tim Urban theorizes that the chronic procrastinator is really a rational decision-maker who tries to coexist with a pet: the instant gratification monkey.

> The Instant Gratification Monkey is the last creature who should be in charge of decisions—he thinks *only* about the present, ignoring lessons from the past and disregarding the future altogether, and he concerns himself entirely with maximizing the ease and pleasure of the current moment. He doesn't understand the Rational Decision-Maker any better than the Rational Decision-Maker understands him—why would we continue doing this jog, he thinks, when we could stop, which would feel better. Why would we practice that instrument when it's not fun? Why would we ever use a computer for work when the internet is sitting right there waiting to be played with? He thinks humans are insane.
>
> In the monkey world, he's got it all figured out—if you eat when you're hungry, sleep when you're tired, and don't do anything difficult, you're a pretty successful monkey. The problem for the procrastinator is that he happens to live in the human world, making the Instant Gratification Monkey a highly unqualified navigator.[*]

The returned Jewish exiles had never heard of the instant gratification monkey, but they had put their own "ease and pleasure" above the task of rebuilding of the Lord's temple.

---

[*]Tim Urban, "Why Procrastinators Procrastinate," *Wait But Why* (blog), October 30, 2013, http://waitbutwhy.com/2013/10/why-procrastinators-procrastinate.html.

Group Discussion. How do you decide what is most important?

Personal Reflection. How satisfied are you with your priorities?

After Persia conquered Babylon, King Cyrus decreed that the exiled Jews could return to their homeland and rebuild the ruined temple of the Lord (Ezra 1:1-4). Thousands of Jews made the journey. Even before they began to rebuild the temple, they built a new altar and resumed the appointed sacrifices according to the law (Ezra 3:1-6). In 536 BC the foundation was laid for a new temple, although one less grand than Solomon's (Ezra 3:7-13). Opposition arose, and the Jews stopped work for about sixteen years until the second year of King Darius (Ezra 4:1-5, 24). At that time the prophet Haggai received the word of the Lord. *Read Haggai 1:1-11.*

1. As Haggai's prophecy begins, what problem is immediately obvious?

2. Consider the Lord's question in verse 3. Why is "no" the only reasonable answer?

3. About five hundred years earlier, King David desired to build a house for the Lord. He thought it wasn't right that he lived in a cedar palace while the ark of God resided in a tent (2 Samuel 7:1-2). How did the attitude of the returned exiles differ from that of David (v. 4)?

4. What are some possible reasons the returned exiles had neglected the work on the temple?

5. What does it mean today to build up the house (or temple) of the Lord?

6. What causes Christians to neglect active involvement in ministry, whether to non-Christians or to each other?

7. In Haggai's time, how did the Lord discipline the people for their neglect of his house (vv. 5-11)?

8. How do you think the people complained about the results of the Lord's discipline?

9. Through Haggai the Lord twice said, "Give careful thought to your ways" (vv. 5, 7). Consider your own local church fellowship. What specific things are happening among you that help build up the Lord's house?

10. What is happening in your own life—whether through involvement in ministries of your church, in the wider community, or on your own—to build up the Lord's house?

11. *Read Haggai 1:12-15.* The Lord assured the people that he was with them in the building effort, and he stirred up the spirits of the leaders Zerubbabel and Joshua. How did the people respond?

12. If Haggai were to talk to you about your involvement in building up the Lord's house, what do you think he would say?

13. What steps will you take to evaluate what you are doing (or failing to do) for the Lord?

Pray for a calm spirit as you evaluate ways you are neglecting the building up of the Lord's house, whether through laziness or through over-busyness. Ask the Lord for wisdom to make needed changes in your priorities and to follow through with your decisions.

NOW OR LATER

The aim of this study is not to get you to sign up for every volunteer opportunity you see in the church bulletin. You may already be *too* involved in so many activities that you need to step back and reevaluate what you are doing and why you are doing it. Consider which activities build up the Lord's house and which are busywork or could be done better by someone else.

Look back on the history of your own church fellowship, as far as you are aware of it. Also look back on the history of your own spiritual life. Have you had times of more active and focused involvement in ministry that have faded away? If so, what happened, and how might that energy for ministry be restored?

LEADER'S NOTES

My grace is sufficient for you.

2 CORINTHIANS 12:9

Leading a Bible discussion can be an enjoyable and rewarding experience. But it can also be scary—especially if you've never done it before. If this is your feeling, you're in good company. When God asked Moses to lead the Israelites out of Egypt, he replied, "Please send someone else" (Exodus 4:13)! It was the same with Solomon, Jeremiah, and Timothy, but God helped these people in spite of their weaknesses, and he will help you as well.

You don't need to be an expert on the Bible or a trained teacher to lead a Bible discussion. The idea behind these inductive studies is that the leader guides group members to discover for themselves what the Bible has to say. This method of learning will allow group members to remember much more of what is said than a lecture would.

These studies are designed to be led easily. As a matter of fact, the flow of questions through the passage from observation to interpretation to application is so natural that you may feel that the studies lead themselves. This study guide is also flexible. You can use it with a variety of groups—student, professional, neighborhood, or church groups. Each study takes forty-five to sixty minutes in a group setting.

There are some important facts to know about group dynamics and encouraging discussion. The suggestions listed below should enable you to effectively and enjoyably fulfill your role as leader.

PREPARING FOR THE STUDY

1. Ask God to help you understand and apply the passage in your own life. Unless this happens, you will not be prepared to lead others. Pray too for the various members of the group. Ask God to open your hearts to the message of his Word and motivate you to action.

2. Read the introduction to the guide to get an overview of the entire book and the issues that will be explored.

3. As you begin each study, read and re-read the assigned Bible passage to familiarize yourself with it.

4. This study guide is based on the New International Version of the Bible. It will help you and the group if you use this translation as the basis for your study and discussion.

5. Carefully work through each question in the study. Spend time in meditation and reflection as you consider how to respond.

6. Write your thoughts and responses in the space provided in the study guide. This will help you to express your understanding of the passage clearly.

7. It might help to have a Bible dictionary handy. Use it to look up any unfamiliar words, names, or places. (For additional help on how to study a passage, see chapter five of *How to Lead a LifeGuide Bible Study*, InterVarsity Press.)

8. Consider how you can apply the Scripture to your life. Remember that the group will follow your lead in responding to the studies. They will not go any deeper than you do.

9. Once you have finished your own study of the passage, familiarize yourself with the leader's notes for the study you are leading. These are designed to help you in several ways. First, they tell you the purpose the study guide author had in mind when writing the study. Take time to think through how the study questions work together to accomplish that purpose. Second, the notes provide you with additional background information or suggestions on group dynamics for various questions. This information can be useful when people have difficulty understanding or answering a question. Third, the leader's notes can alert you to potential problems you may encounter during the study.

10. If you wish to remind yourself of anything mentioned in the leader's notes, make a note to yourself below that question in the study.

LEADING THE STUDY

1. Begin the study on time. Open with prayer, asking God to help the group to understand and apply the passage.

2. Be sure that everyone in your group has a study guide. Encourage the group to prepare beforehand for each discussion by reading the introduction to the guide and by working through the questions in the study.

3. At the beginning of your first time together, explain that these studies are meant to be discussions, not lectures. Encourage the members of the group to participate. However, do not put pressure on those who may be hesitant to speak during the first few sessions. You may want to suggest the following guidelines to your group.

- Stick to the topic being discussed.

- Your responses should be based on the verses that are the focus of the discussion and not on outside authorities such as commentaries or speakers.

- These studies focus on a particular passage of Scripture. Only rarely should you refer to other portions of the Bible. This allows for everyone to participate in in-depth study on equal ground.

- Anything said in the group is considered confidential and will not be discussed outside the group unless specific permission is given to do so.

- We will listen attentively to each other and provide time for each person present to talk.

- We will pray for each other.

4. Have a group member read the introduction at the beginning of the discussion.

5. Every session begins with a group discussion question. The question or activity is meant to be used before the passage is read. The question introduces the theme of the study and encourages group members to begin to open up. Encourage as many members as possible to participate, and be ready to get the discussion going with your own response.

This section is designed to reveal where our thoughts or feelings need to be transformed by Scripture. That is why it is especially important not to read the passage before the discussion question is asked. The passage will tend to color the honest reactions people would otherwise give because they are, of course, supposed to think the way the Bible does.

You may want to supplement the group discussion question with an icebreaker to help people get comfortable. See the community section of *Small Group Idea Book* for more ideas.

You also might want to use the personal reflection question with your group. Either allow a time of silence for people to respond individually or discuss it together.

6. Have a group member (or members if the passage is long) read aloud the passage to be studied. Then give people several minutes to read the passage again silently so that they can take it all in.

7. Question 1 will generally be an overview question designed to briefly survey the passage. Encourage the group to look at the whole passage, but try to avoid getting sidetracked by questions or issues that will be addressed later in the study.

8. As you ask the questions, keep in mind that they are designed to be used just as they are written. You may simply read them aloud. Or you may prefer to express them in your own words.

There may be times when it is appropriate to deviate from the study guide. For example, a question may have already been answered. If so, move on to the next question. Or someone may raise an important question not covered in the guide. Take time to discuss it, but try to keep the group from going off on tangents.

9. Avoid answering your own questions. If necessary, repeat or rephrase them until they are clearly understood. Or point out something you read in the leader's notes to clarify the context or meaning. An eager group quickly becomes passive and silent if they think the leader will do most of the talking.

10. Don't be afraid of silence. People may need time to think about the question before formulating their answers.

11. Don't be content with just one answer. Ask, "What do the rest of you think?" or "Anything else?" until several people have given answers to the question.

12. Acknowledge all contributions. Try to be affirming whenever possible. Never reject an answer. If it is clearly off base, ask, "Which verse led you to that conclusion?" or again, "What do the rest of you think?"

13. Don't expect every answer to be addressed to you, even though this will probably happen at first. As group members become more at ease, they will begin to truly interact with each other. This is one sign of healthy discussion.

14. Don't be afraid of controversy. It can be very stimulating. If you don't resolve an issue completely, don't be frustrated. Move on and keep it in mind for later. A subsequent study may solve the problem.

15. Periodically summarize what the group has said about the passage. This helps to draw together the various ideas mentioned and gives continuity to the study. But don't preach.

16. At the end of the Bible discussion you may want to allow group members a time of quiet to work on an idea under "Now or Later." Then discuss what you experienced. Or you may want to encourage group members to work on these ideas between meetings. Give an opportunity during the session for people to talk about what they are learning.

17. Conclude your time together with conversational prayer, adapting the prayer suggestion at the end of the study to your group. Ask for God's help in following through on the commitments you've made.

18. End on time.

Many more suggestions and helps are found in *How to Lead a LifeGuide Bible Study*.

COMPONENTS OF SMALL GROUPS

A healthy small group should do more than study the Bible. There are four components to consider as you structure your time together.

Nurture. Small groups help us to grow in our knowledge and love of God. Bible study is the key to making this happen and is the foundation of your small group.

Community. Small groups are a great place to develop deep friendships with other Christians. Allow time for informal interaction before and after each study. Plan activities and games that will help you get to know each other. Spend time having fun together going on a picnic or cooking dinner together.

Worship and prayer. Your study will be enhanced by spending time praising God together in prayer or song. Pray for each other's needs and keep track of how God is answering prayer in your group. Ask God to help you to apply what you are learning in your study.

Outreach. Reaching out to others can be a practical way of applying what you are learning, and it will keep your group from becoming self-focused. Host a series of evangelistic discussions for your friends or neighbors. Clean up the yard of an elderly friend. Serve at a soup kitchen together, or spend a day working on a Habitat house.

Many more suggestions and helps in each of these areas are found in Small Group Idea Book. Information on building a small group can be found in *Small Group Leaders' Handbook* and *The Big Book on Small Groups* (both from InterVarsity Press). Reading through one of these books would be worth your time.

Before each study, you may want to put an asterisk by the key questions you think are most important for your group to cover, in case you don't have time to cover all the questions. As we suggested in "Getting the Most Out of *Questions God Asks*," if you want to make sure you have enough time to discuss all the questions, you have other options. For example, the group could decide to extend each meeting to ninety minutes or more. Alternatively, you could devote two sixty-minute sessions to each study.

STUDY 1. WHERE ARE YOU? GENESIS 3:1-13.

PURPOSE: To become increasingly honest about our spiritual state in relation to God.

Question 1. Both the man and the woman are hiding, and the woman is involved in the conversation later. God also asks several follow-up questions. However, this study concentrates specifically on God's first question.

"In Genesis 3 the man recedes as the woman and the snake engage in conversation and then action. Only at the conclusion in Genesis 3:6 does the ʾādām participate. Even then it is a passive role in which he receives and eats what the woman has given him. Yet it is to the ʾādām (Gen 3:9) that God calls. He is the one who first confesses the shame of nakedness that the fruit has now enabled him and the woman to experience" (Richard S. Hess, "Adam," in *Dictionary of the Old Testament: Pentateuch*, ed. T. Desmond Alexander and David W. Baker [Downers Grove, IL: InterVarsity Press, 2002], 20).

"The Fall is immediate upon eating the forbidden tree, as Adam and Eve at once know that they are naked (Gen 3:7) and fear the sound of God walking in the garden (Gen 3:8). The impulse to cover themselves and to hide from God embodies the essential change that has occurred, encompassing shame, self-consciousness, the experience of loss and the awareness of separation from God" ("Fall from Innocence," in *Dictionary of Biblical Imagery*, ed. Leland Ryken, James C. Wilhoit, and Tremper Longman III [Downers Grove, IL: InterVarsity Press, 1998], 263).

Question 3. Similar to the English word *call*, the Hebrew word means "to call out loudly" in order to get someone's attention, "to call out a warning," "to shout," "to proclaim," or "to summon." It can also mean "to name," as in Genesis 2:19 where Adam named the animals. (W. E. Vine, Merrill F. Unger, and William White Jr., "To Call," in *Vine's Complete Expository Dictionary of Old and New Testament Words* [Nashville: Thomas Nelson, 1996], 29-30.)

Question 4. Follow-up questions: Though Adam was physically still in Eden, where was he spiritually, emotionally, relationally? What might it have been like for Adam to feel fear, shame, and guilt for the first time?

Question 6. Follow-up questions: What is God still doing? What is Adam still able to do?

God is still talking to human beings, and human beings can answer. They don't have true communion, but at least they have communication. Adam has not lost his capacity to be honest with God.

Question 8. Possible responses: a record of good works; busyness, including many good activities; a sense of self-righteousness; a plea of ignorance.

STUDY 2. WHAT IS THAT IN YOUR HAND? EXODUS 4:1-5.

PURPOSE: To take stock of our resources and allow the Lord to use them to fulfill our calling from him.

Group Discussion and Personal Reflection. While a better question might be "When have you *not* felt inadequate?" these questions will help identify some ways participants feel weak or overwhelmed.

Question 3. As yet there is no apparent connection between Moses' objection and God's question. Moses must have been mystified about why the Lord called attention to the staff in his hand.

Question 4. In itself there was nothing remarkable about Moses' staff. Shepherds used (and still use) staffs as ordinary tools of their work. No doubt Moses had made this one and had worn out many others over the years.

"*Staff* is the customary biblical term for the walker's stick that was apparently universal in the ancient world. It is thus an icon of the traveler, symbolic of a transitory lifestyle and the vulnerability of living on the road (inasmuch as the staff was used as both a weapon and a support for the weary)" ("Rod, Staff," in *Dictionary of Biblical Imagery*, ed. Leland Ryken, James C. Wilhoit, and Tremper Longman III [Downers Grove, IL: InterVarsity Press, 1998], 733).

The staff was a "stick cut from the stem or branch of a tree and used for numerous purposes. Straight staffs, thicker at one end than at the other and of varying lengths, were the protection and support of shepherds and travelers on foot. They might also serve as poles for carrying burdens, as shafts for arrows or spears, and as instruments for inflicting punishment. A shorter staff with a knobbed end, often studded with nails or bits of flint, served the soldier and the shepherd as a weapon" (Lawrence E. Toombs, "Rod," in *The Interpreter's Dictionary of the Bible*, ed. George Arthur Buttrick et al. [Nashville: Abingdon Press, 1962], 4:102).

Question 5. "The fact that [Moses' staff] was called the staff of God (Ex 4:20; 17:9) indicates that it was not to be conceived magically but as an instrument of God's will (cf. Deut 18:10-12). . . . The fact that God's will was being executed through the staff of God means that the turning of this staff into a snake (Ex 7:10) was of a fundamentally different nature from what the Egyptian magicians did by their secret arts, . . . a fact demonstrated by their rods being swallowed up by Aaron's rod" (Cornelis Van Dam, "Rod, Staff," in *Dictionary of the Old Testament: Pentateuch*, ed. T. Desmond Alexander and David W. Baker [Downers Grove, IL: InterVarsity Press, 2002], 693-94).

Question 6. After forty years in the desert, Moses was very familiar with the dangerous snakes that hid in the rocks. If he picked up a snake at all—which he probably wouldn't—he would grasp it behind the head, not by the tail, where it could twist around and bite him. For Moses to take that snake by the tail, he had to have faith in God and the certainty that he was really hearing from God.

Question 7. "The three signs the Lord gave to Moses each most likely had symbolic significance. The rod was the symbol of authority in Egypt, and Pharaoh was represented by the serpent figure, the uraeus [an upright cobra], featured prominently on his crown. The first sign then suggests that Pharaoh and his authority are completely in the power of God" (John H. Walton, Victor H. Matthews, and Mark W. Chavalas, *The IVP Bible Background Commentary: Old Testament* [Downers Grove, IL: InterVarsity Press, 2000], 80).

Questions 9 and 10. While the Lord may not use every ordinary thing in our lives to do miracles or to do something on the scale of the exodus, this is a good place to consider the means we have, which the Lord might use in unexpected ways. Note that by Exodus 4:20, Moses' staff has become "the staff of God."

Question 11. This is not a question to be answered immediately or lightly, but it will prod participants to think and pray with the aim of getting specific with the Lord.

STUDY 3. WHY ARE YOU CRYING OUT TO ME? EXODUS 14:5-25.

PURPOSE: To develop courage and faith to take action when prompted by the Lord.

Question 2. It looked like there were only two options: death or return to slavery. It was up to Pharaoh which one happened. Pharaoh could have the Israelites immediately slaughtered, or he could have them rounded up and returned to Egypt, where their conditions likely would have been worse than before.

Question 9. Besides death or recapture, a third alternative opened up in front of the Israelites: a safe passage through the sea. They could now obey God's command through Moses to "move on." When they had safely reached the other side, the water closed on the pursuing Egyptian army. The Israelites could continue on their journey toward the land of promise with no further threat from Egypt.

Note that boldly moving forward is not always what God desires. In this session's Scripture, the Israelites moved forward in obedience to the word of the Lord through Moses. At other times they moved forward in *dis*obedience to the word of the Lord, with disastrous results. A striking example is in Numbers 14. When most of the spies who scouted out

Canaan came back with a discouraging report, the Israelites rebelled and talked of stoning Moses and Aaron and heading back to Egypt. The Lord declared that that generation would never enter the land of promise. The people then changed their minds and went charging toward Canaan, only to be repulsed by the local inhabitants.

Question 10. Depending on participants' backgrounds and experiences, answers will vary: Scripture in general, specific passages in Scripture brought to one's attention at key moments, listening in prayer, advice from wise counselors, circumstances, unexplained coincidences, visions, inner certainty, promptings during worship, and other possible avenues of hearing from God.

At two extremes, some Christians believe that God's will is always a perfect "dot" or target we must hit, while others believe that within his moral guidelines God gives us a wide scope of choices. Other views lie somewhere in-between.

We can be sure that God's will for us will never contradict Scripture. For example, a person in an unhappy marriage does not need to ask God "Should I have an extramarital affair?" because that option is already ruled out by Scripture.

Question 11. Moses lived in such closeness with God that he knew without a doubt when God told him to move forward. Clear guidance from the Lord comes out of a trusting relationship with him.

"God's ultimate will is that we know Him, love Him, glorify Him, and grow in an intimate relationship with Him. I have repeated that for emphasis because it is out of this supreme purpose that specifics are given us. He longs for us to live in close fellowship with Him; He is constantly invading our lives, wanting to guide our every thought, reaction, and decision. He is not aloof, hiding until we say or do the right things to unlock His will. He has come in Jesus Christ to do all that is necessary to transform our minds and liberate our wills to want His will" (Lloyd John Ogilvie, *Discovering God's Will in Your Life* [Eugene, OR: Harvest House, 1982], 22-23).

STUDY 4. STAND UP! WHAT ARE YOU DOING DOWN ON YOUR FACE? JOSHUA 7:1-15.

PURPOSE: To take responsibility where it is appropriate, rather than merely complain to the Lord.

Question 2. Falling on one's face was a typical response to meeting with the Lord, for example Abram in Genesis 17:3 and Samson's parents in Judges 13:20. Sometimes the Lord or an angel immediately commanded the person to stand up because there was a message for the person: for example, Ezekiel 1:28–2:3; Daniel 8:15-19; and implied in Revelation 1:17-18. In Joshua's case, however, something different is going on when the Lord commands him to stand up.

Question 3. These are some possible paraphrases of Joshua's prayer:

- God, why did you put us in this situation?
- If only we'd been content with the way things were.
- We've lost the battle; we're defeated.
- We're doomed; we're without hope.
- Lord, this will destroy your reputation.

Question 5. God has made us physical as well as spiritual beings. Small physical actions can have big psychological effects. If you don't want to get out of bed, just swinging your legs over and putting your feet on the floor will get you started. Turn a doorknob, pick up a phone, put a dollar in an offering plate, open a book, say hello to a neighbor, pick up a dust rag—the smallest actions can lead to a change of attitude and payoff in tangible results.

Question 6. The sins certainly include covetousness, theft, and lying; but most serious was disobeying the Lord's command to destroy Jericho and to "keep away from the devoted things, so that you will not bring about your own destruction by taking any of them" (Joshua 6:18).

"The best analogy for us to understand *herem* [the command of total destruction] is to think in terms of radiation. A nuclear explosion would destroy many things and irradiate much more. The abhorrence and caution with which we would respond to that which has been irradiated is similar to what is expected of the Israelites regarding things under the ban. If radiation were personified, one could understand that once something was given over to it, it was irredeemable. It was this condition that Achan exposed himself to by taking things under the ban" (John H. Walton, Victor H. Matthews, and Mark W. Chavalas, *The IVP Bible Background Commentary: Old Testament* [Downers Grove, IL: InterVarsity Press, 2000], 218).

Question 8. The point of this question is not to engage in condemnation but to see how individual sin affects a widening circle of people. Discourage participants from talking about local situations. Unfortunately, there are many well-known incidents of Christian leaders who fell into sin and consequently damaged or even destroyed their ministries.

STUDY 5. WHAT ARE YOU DOING HERE? 1 KINGS 19:1-18.

PURPOSE: To gain courage to face difficult situations with the Lord's strength, rather than trying to escape them.

Question 2. Follow-up question: Does Elijah feel like a failure? Why or why not?

We do not know the identity of Elijah's "ancestors" (v. 4). The Bible tells us nothing about his background except that he was a "Tishbite, from Tishbe in Gilead" (1 Kings 17:1). Apparently he considered himself to be no better than them.

Jill Briscoe offers these impressions of Elijah: "I have a sense that Elijah was an intense sort of man, a perfectionist, an overachiever. He probably expected an enormous amount from himself. . . . It's galling for the overachiever to know that no one who came before him did all of it right, and he won't do all of it right either! But he won't do all of it wrong. Some of it will be wrong, but not all of it. Remember that we are fallen, so at best we can only be the best, fallen . . . Christian servant we can be.

"It sounds as if Elijah was comparing himself with his forebears and was coming to terms with this very thing. He was feeling that he had failed just as they had failed. He wanted to be better than his ancestors, because, I suspect, Elijah wanted to be better than everybody, and when he found out he was just like everyone else, he couldn't take it. . . . When you become desperately disappointed with yourself, it can land you flat on your face, like Elijah. But that is often an ideal place to begin to lower your expectations of yourself and get a more realistic view of life" (Jill Briscoe, *Prayer That Works* [Wheaton, IL: Tyndale House, 2000], 131).

Question 3. The Lord knew what Elijah needed and mercifully fulfilled three basic necessities for him: food, water, and rest. When troubles exhaust us, we often overlook these fundamental needs, and as a result we only exhaust ourselves further.

Question 8. Elijah has apparently retreated back inside the cave, for he again comes to the cave mouth, his face covered by his cloak. John Wesley wrote that Elijah covered his face "through dread of God's presence, being sensibly that he was neither worthy nor able to endure the sight of God with open face" (John Wesley, "John Wesley's Explanatory Notes," Christianity.com, www.christianity.com/bible/commentary .php?com=wes&b=11&c=19).

The fact that there is no difference between Elijah's answers in verses 10 and 14 may show that he has not changed his mind about his situation.

Question 10. "The gods of the ancient Near East do not have a plan that they reveal. While they are believed to be active throughout the scope of history, there is no indication that they had a plan for the direction of history. Here it is made plain to Elijah that Yahweh is not simply a hot-blooded warrior defending or dethroning kings on an arbitrary whim like the gods of the ancient Near East. He has an agenda for history. His warfare is not just wrathful blood-letting—there is a long-term plan that is being carefully worked out" (John H. Walton, Victor H. Matthews, and Mark W. Chavalas, *The IVP Bible Background Commentary: Old Testament* [Downers Grove, IL: InterVarsity Press, 2000], 380).

STUDY 6. WHY DO YOU COMPLAIN, JACOB? ISAIAH 40:27-31; 41:8-10.

PURPOSE: To grow in trust that the Lord cares about our difficulties, even those we have brought on ourselves.

Question 2. The land of Judah, and specifically the city of Jerusalem, were the center of Jewish identity. God's temple and therefore God's presence were in Jerusalem. Now the city and temple were in ruins, and the Jews had been forcibly marched hundreds of miles away from their homeland. No wonder they felt they had been sent away from the very presence of God. There are two parts to their plea: they are hidden from God (he can't find them), and their cause is disregarded by God (he does not care).

Question 3. Though they felt that God was disregarding them, they had first disregarded him through their persistent idolatry. Still the Lord expressed his concern and his determination to come to their aid.

Question 4. As Christian believers we want to say—and feel we should say—that we're sure the Lord always hears and cares. Perhaps some

Christians always feel such confidence, but most of us experience times when we wonder if God cares about what we are going through. Responding to this question requires courageous honesty, both to admit that we sometimes feel God doesn't care and that sometimes our troubles are our own fault.

Question 5. The people accused God of ignoring them. But far from ignoring them, God spoke to them directly (through Isaiah) and kept up active communication with them. He persistently invited their response to his questions.

Question 6. "In the ancient world the gods were viewed as having human weaknesses and often were inattentive or simply unaware of events that were taking place. One result of this was that the pantheon of gods were constantly outwitting or tricking each other. . . . The gods were not indefatigable. They were in constant need of food, drink and shelter. In fact, humans were created to do the hard labor the gods preferred not to do" (John H. Walton, Victor H. Matthews, and Mark W. Chavalas, *The IVP Bible Background Commentary: Old Testament* [Downers Grove, IL: InterVarsity Press, 2000], 627).

In contrast to the false gods, the Lord "will not grow tired or weary" (v. 28).

Question 7. The promise that the exiles will "soar on wings like eagles" (v. 31) makes use of a powerful biblical image for God's intervention on behalf of his people.

"The eagle symbolizes the speed and power of both God's deliverance and God's destruction. Speaking of how he delivered Israel from Egypt, the Lord says, 'You yourselves have seen what I did to Egypt, and how I carried you on eagles' wings and brought you to myself' (Ex 19:4 NIV). Similar images of God's protection as an eagle, swift and powerful, are found in Deuteronomy 32:11 and Revelation 12:14" ("Eagle," in *Dictionary of Biblical Imagery*, ed. Leland Ryken, James C. Wilhoit, and Tremper Longman III [Downers Grove, IL: InterVarsity Press, 1998], 223).

STUDY 7. CAN THESE BONES LIVE? EZEKIEL 37:1-14.

PURPOSE: To grow in hope that the Lord will work out his purposes even in seemingly hopeless situations.

Question 7. "In the Genesis account of Creation man was a lifeless, inert being until the breath or spirit of God was breathed into him; then he became a living soul. The difference between life and death, according to the prophet, was to be found in the presence of God's spirit in individual or corporate life.... In the Valley of Dry Bones vision (ch. 37), the concept that God makes the difference between life and death is graphically described.... The prophet saw a vision of a valley filled with dry, bleached bones, presumably a battlefield where the fallen warriors of the defeated were never buried. In all probability such desolate regions had been known by exiled Ezekiel, who had seen his own land reduced to death. The Almighty asks the question: 'Can these bones live?' Hope had been all but extinguished among the exiles. Was there any reason for hope? God then answered with action. Ezekiel would prophesy, and the spirit of God would breathe or blow upon the death-filled valley and in doing so would raise the fallen army once more to be a mighty host. ... The prophet left nothing to the imagination of the reader, pointing out that the vision meant that God would restore his people Israel, who were now as dead, and make them live again" (Carl G. Howie, "Ezekiel," in *The Interpreter's Dictionary of the Bible*, ed. George Arthur Buttrick et al. [Nashville: Abingdon Press, 1962], 2:209-10).

Question 8. "The popular theological notion of the day was that Jerusalem, being God's dwelling place, was inviolate against attack. This concept had been fostered by the defeat of Sennacherib in 701 B.C. and the prophecies of Isaiah ben Amoz in connection therewith. Yahweh's city was Jerusalem, and the temple was his house which no enemy could ever conquer or profane. When, therefore, the temple was destroyed and Jerusalem was reduced to rubble, the popular faith of Israel was dealt a blow from which the people would not have recovered had it not been for the prophetic voice and word. To the average Hebrew, God had been defeated, his land conquered, and his people scattered. The foundation of faith had thus been shattered almost beyond repair" (Howie, "Ezekiel," 2:209-10).

Question 10. "Yahweh's action is not to be understood as healing and raising up a people who in itself still possesses something of a possibility for and right to life. It is the resurrection from a justly imposed death, and the creator of life alone can make it possible. In all this the meaning is not individual resurrection but . . . a restoration of the community to their homeland" (Walther Theodor Zimmerli, "Ezekiel," in *The Interpreter's Dictionary of the Bible*, ed. Keith Crim et al., sup. ed. [Nashville: Abingdon Press, 1976], 316).

Question 11. In the dry bones of Ezekiel's valley, John Wesley saw a picture of his own hopeless efforts to produce love for God through the power of his own reasoning. Reason, Wesley wrote, "may present us with fair ideas; it can draw a fine picture of love: But this is only a painted fire. And farther than this reason cannot go. I made the trial for many years. I collected the finest hymns, prayers, and meditations which I could find in any language; and I said, sung, or read them over and over, with all possible seriousness and attention. But still I was like the bones in Ezekiel's vision: 'The skin covered them above; but there was no breath in them'" (John Wesley, "The Case of Reason Impartially Considered," sermon 70, *SAGE Digital Library*, vol. 1-4 [Albany, OR: SAGE Software, 1996], 398).

STUDY 8. IS IT RIGHT FOR YOU TO BE ANGRY? JONAH 4:1-11.

PURPOSE: To let go of self-righteous anger and grow in mercy as the Lord is merciful.

Question 1. Jonah 1:1 identifies "Jonah son of Amittai" but does not give any clues about when he lived. Second Kings 14:25 refers to "Jonah son of Amittai, the prophet from Gath Hepher." This was during the reign of Jeroboam II, king of Israel in the eighth century BC. It appears to be the same person.

Jonah fled to the seaport of Joppa to escape preaching to the Assyrians, who were Gentile pagans. It is interesting that Joppa is the place where Peter received the revelation that the gospel is also for the Gentiles (Acts 10).

Question 5. If it is difficult to admit to being *angry*, an alternative word is *touchy*. Note that we can be angry at ourselves for our own sin, as well as angry at others for their sin.

Question 6. It is appropriate to be compassionately angry when we see people hurt and victimized, especially when such feelings stir us to action to come to the victims' aid. Anger that rises from a sense of wounded self-righteousness is harder to justify.

Question 7. "The plant that brings Jonah shade is described by a general term usually associated with the gourd family. As with the fish [Jonah 1:17–2:1, 10], the terminology does not allow a more specific identification. The insect that destroys the gourd plant is most likely of the aphid variety" (John H. Walton, Victor H. Matthews, and Mark W. Chavalas, *The IVP Bible Background Commentary: Old Testament* [Downers Grove, IL: InterVarsity Press, 2000], 780).

Question 11. Concerning God's mercy toward Nineveh, John Calvin wrote, "Why did the Lord send Jonah to the Ninevites to predict the overthrow of their city? Why did he by Isaiah give Hezekiah intimation of his death? He might have destroyed both them and him without a message to announce the disaster. He had something else in view than to give them a warning of death, which might let them see it at a distance before it came. It was because he did not wish them destroyed but reformed, and thereby saved from destruction. When Jonah prophesies that in forty days Nineveh will be overthrown, he does it in order to prevent the overthrow. When Hezekiah is forbidden to hope for longer life, it is that he may obtain longer life. Who does not now see that, by threatening of this kind, God wished to arouse those to repentance whom he terrified, that they might escape the judgment which their sins deserved?" (John Calvin, "Use to Be Made of the Doctrine of Providence," in *Institutes of the Christian Religion* [Albany, OR: SAGE Software, 1996], 259).

Question 12. "Assyrian scholars have estimated the population of Nineveh (city and surrounding countryside) when it was the capital city at about three hundred thousand, so the hundred and twenty thousand here for an earlier period is not implausible" (John H. Walton, Victor H. Matthews, and Mark W. Chavalas, *The IVP Bible Background Commentary: Old Testament* [Downers Grove, IL: InterVarsity Press, 2000], 780).

STUDY 9. IS IT A TIME FOR YOU YOURSELVES TO BE LIVING IN YOUR PANELED HOUSES, WHILE THIS HOUSE REMAINS A RUIN? HAGGAI 1:1-15.

PURPOSE: To reevaluate what is most important and to put building the kingdom of God in its rightful first place.

Question 1. Although there had been opposition from the enemies of the Jews, Haggai's prophecy does not mention opposition. Apparently at this point the work on the temple was at a standstill for other reasons. It is striking that the people were saying "the time has not yet come" even though there was already momentum underway, a new altar had been built, and the foundation of a new temple had been laid amid great celebration (Ezra 3).

The governor Zerubbabel was descended from the exiled King Jehoiachin, Judah's last king of the Davidic line (2 Kings 25:27-30; 1 Chronicles 3:17-19). Zerubbabel and the high priest Joshua are often mentioned together as joint receivers of Haggai's words from the Lord.

Question 2. "The term *paneled* can mean 'covered,' 'roofed,' or 'paneled,' but the point in any case is that it represents the finishing touches. Their homes were not 'in process' but were fully appointed, while the temple remained a ruin. The term does not imply luxury or great expense, though paneling can be of that nature" (John H. Walton, Victor H. Matthews, and Mark W. Chavalas, *The IVP Bible Background Commentary: Old Testament* [Downers Grove, IL: InterVarsity Press, 2000], 797).

Question 4. In his commentary on Haggai, John Calvin wrote, "As liberty to build the Temple was given to the Jews, we may gather from what our Prophet says, that they were guilty of ingratitude towards God; for private benefit was by every one almost exclusively regarded, and there was hardly any concern for the worship of God. Hence the Prophet now reproves this indifference, allied as it was with ungodliness: for what could be more base than to enjoy the country and the inheritance which God had formerly promised to Abraham, and yet to make no account of God, nor of that special favour which he wished to confer—that of dwelling among them? An habitation on mount Sion had been chosen, we know, by God, that thence might come forth the Redeemer of the world. As then this business was neglected, and each one built his own house, justly does the Prophet here reprove them with vehemence in the name and by the command of God. . . . The Jews were negligent, because they were too much devoted to their own private advantages" (John Calvin, *Commentaries on the Twelve Minor Prophets*, trans. John Owen, vol. 4 [Grand Rapids: Eerdmans, 1950], www.iclnet.org/pub /resources/text/m.sion/cvhag-02.htm).

Question 5. Possible follow-up question: "What is the temple of the Lord today?" Believers in Christ are called the temple or house of the

Holy Spirit (1 Corinthians 3:16-17; 6:19; 2 Corinthians 6:16; Ephesians 2:19-21; Hebrews 3:6). To build up the Lord's house today can mean leading more people to have faith in Christ as well as encouraging the faith and obedience of believers.

Question 6. The most succinct answer is what Jesus called "the desires for other things" (Mark 4:19). More specific answers: lethargy; self-interest; distraction with details of work and family; being overly busy, even with good things; fear of losing status in the world's eyes; and fear of material loss.

Questions 7 and 8. The concept of blessings for obedience and curses for disobedience had been deeply ingrained in Jewish teaching since the time of Moses (Deuteronomy 28). Here the Lord specifically ties neglect of the temple with the futility of the people's plans and endeavors.

Questions 9 and 10. Point out that there are endless possible shapes of ministry. It can take place in a well-established church program or in a groundbreaking new form of outreach or teaching. It can mean venturing thousands of miles away or going next door. The financial cost can range from significant to zero. It may require a large group of people or only a few, or even one. What unifies all these possible forms of ministry is their purpose: to build up the house of the Lord.

Question 11. Bible scholar William Neil says, "It would appear to be largely because of [Haggai's] energy and enthusiasm, as indicated in his oracles, that the work of restoration was begun almost immediately after his first appeal, and completed within four years (Ezra 6:15)" (William Neil, "Haggai," in *The Interpreter's Dictionary of the Bible*, ed. George Arthur Buttrick et al. [Nashville: Abingdon Press, 1962], 2:509).

Questions 12 and 13. Possible follow-up questions: Are there ministry endeavors you began with enthusiasm and then let slide because you lost interest? Why did you lose interest? Which endeavors can and should be revived?

Dale and Sandy Larsen are writers living in Rochester, Minnesota. They have authored over thirty Bible studies, including more than ten LifeGuide® Bible Studies.

What should we study next?

We have LifeGuides for . . .

LifeGuide® BIBLE STUDIES

KNOWING JESUS
Advent of the Savior
Following Jesus
I Am
Abiding in Christ
Jesus' Final Week
The Jesus Paul Knew

KNOWING GOD
Listening to God
Meeting God
God's Comfort
God's Love
The 23rd Psalm
Miracles
Questions God Asks

**GROWING IN
THE SPIRIT**
Meeting the Spirit
Fruit of the Spirit
Spiritual Gifts
Spiritual Warfare

**LOOKING AT
THE TRINITY**
Images of Christ
Images of God
Images of the Spirit

**DEVELOPING
DISCIPLINES**
Christian Disciplines
God's Word
Hospitality
The Lord's Prayer

Prayer
Praying the Psalms
Sabbath
Worship

**DEEPENING
YOUR DOCTRINE**
Angels
Apostles' Creed
Christian Beliefs
The Cross
End Times
Good & Evil
Heaven
The Kingdom of God
The Story of Scripture

SEEKERS
Encountering Jesus
Jesus the Reason
Meeting Jesus
Good News

LEADERS
Christian Leadership
Integrity
Elijah
Joseph

**SHAPING YOUR
CHARACTER**
Christian Character
Decisions
Self-Esteem
Parables
Pleasing God

Woman of God
Women of the
  New Testament
Women of the
  Old Testament

**LIVING FULLY
AT EVERY STAGE**
Singleness
Marriage
Parenting
Couples of the
  Old Testament
Growing Older
  & Wiser
Grandparenting

**REACHING
OUR WORLD**
Missions
Evangelism
Four Great Loves
Loving Justice

LIVING YOUR FAITH
Busyness
Christian Virtues
Forgiveness

**GROWING IN
RELATIONSHIPS**
Christian Community
Friendship

Find the perfect study for your group with IVP's LifeGuide Finder:
ivpress.com/lifeguidefinder